D1472804

# LEADING WOMEN

## *Michelle Obama*

44th First
Lady and
Health and
Education
Advocate

KEZIA ENDSLEY

Cavendish
Square

New York

*To Erik, for everything*

Published in 2015 by Cavendish Square Publishing, LLC
243 5th Avenue, Suite 136, New York, NY 10016

Copyright © 2015 by Cavendish Square Publishing, LLC

First Edition

Library of Congress Cataloging-in-Publication Data

Endsley, Kezia.
Michelle Obama : 44th first lady and health and education advocate / Kezia Endsley.
pages cm. — (Leading women)
Includes bibliographical references and index.
ISBN 978-1-62712-975-6 (hardcover) ISBN 978-1-62712-977-0 (ebook)
1. Obama, Michelle, 1964—-Juvenile literature. 2. Presidents' spouses—United States—Biography—Juvenile literature. 3. Legislators' spouses—United States—Biography—Juvenile literature. 4. African American women lawyers—Illinois—Chicago—Biography—Juvenile literature. 5. African American women—Biography—Juvenile literature. 6. Chicago (Ill.)—Biography—Juvenile literature. I. Title.

E909.O24E53 2014
973.932092—dc23
[B]

2014002026

Editorial Director: Dean Miller
Editor: Andrew Coddington
Senior Copy Editor: Wendy A. Reynolds
Art Director: Jeffrey Talbot
Designer: Amy Greenan/Joseph Macri
Photo Researcher: J8 Media
Production Manager: Jennifer Ryder-Talbot
Production Editor: David McNamara

The photographs in this book are used by permission and through the courtesy of: Cover photo, 1, Official White House Photo by Chuck Kennedy/File:Michelle Obama 2013 official portrait.jpg/ Wikimedia Commons; AP Photo/Ron Edmonds, 4; Keith Levit/Design Pics/Perspectives/Getty Images, 7; Polaris, 9; © Seth Poppel/Yearbook Library, 16; TIM SLOAN/AFP/Getty Images, 21; AP Photo/Mel Evans, 22; Edw. G. van Marter/File:Ivy Club postcard 1909.jpg/Wikimedia Commons, 26; WILLIAM WEST/AFP/Getty Images, 28; Polaris, 33; © iStockphoto.com/ DenisTangneyJr, 34; © Jim Weber/The Commercial Appeal/ZUMAPRESS.com, 41; Polaris, 42; Johner Images/Getty Images, 46; © Jason Reese/age footstock, 49; Apic/Hulton Archive/Getty Images, 52; Polaris, 59; AP Photo/Obama for America, 60; Polaris, 66; AP Photo/Jerry Lai, 70; Scott Olson/Getty Images, 71; Scott Olson/Getty Images, 74; Scott J. Ferrell/CQ-Roll Call Group/Getty Images, 76; Joe Raedle/Getty Images, 81; Pool/Getty Images, 82; Alex Wong/Getty Images, 85.

Printed in the United States of America

# CONTENTS

# CHAPTER ONE

# Growing Up in Chicago

It was August 25, 2008, the first night of the Democratic National **Convention**. The crowd was waiting in anticipation for the next speaker. Michelle Obama—the wife of Barack Obama, who was about to become the **Democratic Party's** nominee for president—appeared on stage. The cheers grew louder. In addition to the live audience, an estimated twenty million television viewers were waiting to hear what she had to say.

Michelle's speech was the sum and substance of who she is. It was a very personal speech about her life, her values, and her family. Her goal was clearly to show the American public who she and Barack were, and that they weren't so different than anyone else. She talked about love of her family, including her mother and brother, who were present that night. She spoke about her beloved father, who passed away in 1990, saying, "I can feel my dad looking down on us, just as I can feel his presence in every grace-filled moment of my life."

She spoke also about her daughters. "I come here as a mom whose girls are the heart of my heart and the center of my world." And, of course, she told the audience about the Barack Obama she knew, the husband and father. Despite his "funny name," she said, he shared her values and principles.

> "Barack and I were raised with so many of the same values, like you work hard for what you want in life. That your word is your bond. That you treat people with dignity and respect, even if you don't agree with them."

Her speech was heartfelt and genuine, and the audience could tell. There weren't many dry eyes in the room when Michelle was done speaking. "Each of us comes here by way of our own improbable journey," she said. Michelle's own improbable journey started on Chicago's south side, in 1964.

## A "South Side" Girl

Michelle LaVaughn Robinson was born the second child of Frasier Robinson III and Marian Shields Robinson in

Chicago, Illinois, on January 17, 1964. She was born and raised on Chicago's south side, which contained a large, thriving African American community. Her parents— Frasier and Marian—rented a small, one-bedroom apartment from Michelle's great aunt. Their home was filled with warmth and lots of extended family.

The Chicago skyline loomed in the background of Michelle Robinson's childhood.

Although the Robinsons didn't have much money, there was a lot of love in their home. Everyone was expected to be at the table every night for dinner, and they participated in lively discussions. On Saturday nights, the family played board games together. Michelle and her older brother Craig were allowed to watch TV only one hour a day, and they were expected to spend their free time reading, playing sports, and otherwise entertaining themselves.

When Michelle and Craig were a bit older, their parents split the living room into two smaller rooms, enabling their children to each have a bedroom and a little personal space to call their own. A lot was expected of Michelle and her brother, but a lot was given in return.

## Learning What's Important: Family and Education

Michelle was born during the height of the **Civil Rights** movement. In fact, during her childhood, the country that her parents knew would slowly begin to change. The Chicago that Michelle was born into was a **segregated** city, and black workers had fewer career opportunities than whites. However, the Civil Rights movement of the 1950s and 1960s helped to bring these issues to the fore and fought to make things better for minorities.

Michelle was exposed to politics at a young age, as her father was a **precinct captain** for the Democratic Party in Chicago. As captain of a precinct, he would canvas its neighborhoods to encourage neighbors to register and to vote for the candidates the party supported, and would often bring young Michelle along with him. He did all this despite the fact that he had **multiple sclerosis** and found it painful to walk even short distances. She saw first-hand at an early age how important politics could be.

"Some of my earliest memories," Michelle has said, "are of tagging along with him as we'd walk door to door and help folks register to vote. We'd sit in neighbors' kitchens for hours and listen to their opinions, their concerns, and the dreams they had for their children. And before we left those kitchens, my father would make sure that everyone could get to the voting booth on Election Day—because he knew that a single vote could help make their dreams a reality."

Although Frasier always said he didn't always completely trust politicians, he knew it was his responsibility to help facilitate the change he wanted to see. It was a key component of the overall philosophy he lived by and taught his children: You can do or be anything you want if you work hard enough and don't give up. There's no room for making excuses.

Michelle learned at a young age that education was the key to success.

As a very young girl, however, Michelle's biggest concern was keeping up with her precocious older brother, Craig. He set the standard to which she aspired. They were twenty-one months apart. When Craig learned to read at the age of four, Michelle wanted to do the same, and when Craig was able to skip second grade, Michelle made it her mission to follow suit. She succeeded in both endeavors.

Keeping up with Craig was a challenge, but the two siblings were friendly rivals. Despite the competition, Michelle and Craig were—and remain—very close. Although she did eventually follow him to New Jersey's Princeton University for her undergraduate education, at some point, their interests diverged. Craig followed his dream and natural abilities to play basketball at Princeton. He is currently the head coach of the men's basketball team at Oregon State.

Years later, in a speech on television, Michelle described Craig as "my mentor, my protector, and my lifelong friend."

## Dreams of Her Own Father

When Michelle was only a year old, her father Frasier was diagnosed with multiple sclerosis, which is a degenerative, autoimmune disease that attacks the central nervous system (the brain and spinal cord). He suffered from muscle tremors and general muscle

## The Jim Crow Laws and the Great Migration

The **Great Migration** was the movement of approximately six million African Americans from the rural South to the North's urban areas. (More than 500,000 ended up in Chicago alone.) The migration spanned about sixty years, from 1910 to 1970. What would cause so many people to leave their homes, families, and ways of life to move to the unknown?

The answer to that question is complicated and varied. One significant reason was the **Jim Crow laws** that prevailed in the American South between 1876 and 1965. These laws mandated the legal separation of blacks and whites. Starting in 1890, African Americans were given "separate but equal" status, which meant that their facilities (including schools, public restrooms and parks, restaurants, drinking fountains, and public transportation) were separate from those for white citizens. These facilities, however, were rarely "equal." These practices also included job discrimination and separation; even the U.S. military was segregated. The weight of this racist segregation was heavy, and it led many African Americans to leave the South with dreams of jobs and equality in the North.

weakness and numbness. Over time, he needed a cane and then crutches to walk, but Michelle never saw or heard him complain. In fact, Frasier was described by neighbors and friends as "always joking," despite his disability. Michelle's dad died unexpectedly after a kidney operation in 1990, when Michelle was just twenty-five. She paid tribute to his perseverance, strength, and determination at the 2008 Democratic National Convention, where she said about her father,

> *"My dad was our rock. He was our champion, our hero."*

Craig and Michelle learned from their father how to work hard, endure hardships, and reach high. His illness did weigh on the two children, and they worried about him. They both felt like they could not let their dad down, because he worked so hard for them, and they saw his pain and the sacrifices he made.

Frasier worked as a water plant pump operator for the Chicago water department, and over the years, he was promoted, eventually becoming the operation engineer. Although he didn't make a lot of money, he provided for his family and enabled Michelle's mother Marian to stay home with their children. "My mother came home and took care of us through high school. My father was a city shift worker who took care of us all his life. The only thing amazing about my life," Michelle has said, "is that a man like my father could raise a family of four on a single city worker's salary."

Despite their father Frasier's battle with multiple sclerosis and the high expectations placed on Craig and Michelle, the household was happy and light-hearted. Both Michelle and Craig always felt loved and special. "When you grow up as a black kid in a white world, people are telling you—sometimes not maliciously, sometimes maliciously—you're not good enough," Craig said. "To have a family, which we did, who constantly reminded you how smart you were, how successful you could be, it's hard to combat. Our parents gave us a little head start by making us feel confident."

Michelle agrees that her parents were always her biggest advocates and pushed her to be her best. She says, "My parents told us time and again, 'Don't tell us what you can't do.'"

Even though they were taught to feel special, they also were expected to take on responsibilities at home, work hard, and earn good grades. Frasier and Marian emphasized hard work and doing your best. Michelle and Craig both had their own alarm clocks long before they started kindergarten, and they were expected to help around the house. Even with the chores and high expectations, Michelle had time for fun and to do the things that normal girls did at that time, including playing with Barbies and cooking with her Easy-Bake Oven.

# Chicago's South Side

For about 100 years, starting in the 1840s, the south side of Chicago was settled by white European immigrants from places like Ireland, Italy, Germany, and Poland. Starting in the early part of the 20th century, during the Great Migration, more than 500,000 African Americans moved to Chicago from the southern United States. Before this migration, African Americans made up two percent of Chicago's population; by 1970, they were 33 percent. They came in part to work in the city's rail yards, steel mills, and meatpacking plants, which were largely located on Chicago's south side. Included in that group was Michelle's great-grandfather, Frasier Robinson, Sr., who came to Chicago from South Carolina looking for a better life. As African Americans began to settle in the south side, the whites moved out. This created a city that was heavily segregated until the 1960s.

Today, the south side covers almost 60 percent of Chicago and is one of the country's largest African American communities. Many middle class families settle in the neighborhoods, although poverty is endemic on the south side as well. It is made up of several neighborhoods, including Hyde Park and South Shore. It is home to the University of Chicago, the Chicago White Sox, Frank Lloyd Wright's house, and numerous artists and writers.

## The Educational Challenge

Although neither of them attended college themselves, Frasier and Marian challenged Michelle and Craig academically at home and placed a premium on the value of education. Michelle and Craig attended Bryn Mawr Elementary School (now called Bouchet Math and Science Academy), which was just around the corner from their apartment. Marian was determined to keep Michelle ahead of her teachers' expectations. "If you aren't challenged, you don't make progress," Marian explained.

The Robinsons didn't just focus on teaching facts and figures; they also encouraged both of their children to think for themselves and to ask questions. Michelle's mother Marian has said, "We told them, 'Make sure you respect your teachers, but don't hesitate to question them.'" Marian has said that she focused on teaching her children it was okay to ask questions because, as a child, she never felt that she was allowed to question her teachers or other adults. As a precocious and bright child herself, she'd found this very frustrating.

Michelle in particular seemed acutely aware of when things weren't fair, and she had a bit of a temper, which sometimes got her into trouble at school. Even when her father explained to her that life is not fair and you don't always get what you deserve, Michelle understood the fairness and equanimity doled out at home and wanted that for all the students at school.

Michelle attended the Whitney M. Young Magnet High School for gifted students in Chicago.

Her brother Craig recalls how Michelle viewed these issues as a young girl, when the two of them would sit up nights talking. "My sister always talked about who was getting picked on at school or who was having a tough time at home. I didn't realize it then but I realize it now: Those were the people she was going to dedicate her life to, the people who were struggling with life's challenges."

From sixth though eighth grade, Michelle was enrolled in Bryn Mawr's gifted program. As part of that program, she was able to take French before most students were exposed to it. She also took a biology class at Kennedy-King Community College, which required her to leave the safe cocoon of her school and travel four miles to the campus. She was learning at this early age to seek out the best education she could find.

After graduating salutatorian (second) in her eighth grade class of over 100 students at Bryn Mawr, she was accepted into the Whitney M. Young Magnet High School, a public high school for Chicago's gifted students. It had opened just two years previously to help erase the city's ethnic and racial boundaries by bringing together gifted students from all backgrounds. The school's academic standards—superior to most every high school in the area—drew competitive, high-achieving Michelle to it.

The school is located in Chicago's West Loop, which was about ten miles from her home. Michelle rode a city bus and the subway each day to get there, a commute that took about an hour and a half each way. She was a devoted and competitive student, taking honors and advanced classes, and made the honor roll every year. She became a member of the National Honor Society, and was elected treasurer of her senior class.

Michelle was five feet eleven inches tall and a very good basketball player, but she did not participate in sports during her high school years. She admits to being too competitive in some respects, which kept her off the court. She also did not want to be compared to Craig, who had been a star basketball player at his high school, Mount Carmel. She instead dedicated herself to her academics. It paid off when she was accepted into the 1985 class of Princeton University, where her brother was a sophomore.

## The Family Legacy

Although Michelle's father Frasier died in 1990 at age fifty-four, she is still greatly influenced by the legacy he left. "I am constantly trying to make sure that I am making him proud," she said, referring to her father during a campaign speech. "What would my father think of the choices that I've made, how I've lived my life, what careers I chose, what man I married? That's the voice in my head that keeps me whole and keeps me grounded."

Michelle's mother Marian followed the Obamas to the White House to help care for Barack and Michelle's

The Civil Rights Act was passed in 1964, the year Michelle was born, and the Voting Rights Act followed the next year.

The Civil Rights Act of 1964 prohibited discrimination on the basis of race, color, religion, sex, or national origin. It ended the Jim Crow laws, which the Supreme Court upheld in 1896 by concluding that "separate but equal" racial segregation was okay. Congress eventually expanded the Civil Rights Act to strengthen enforcement of these fundamental civil rights.

The Voting Rights Act of 1965 banned racial discrimination in voting practices by the federal, state, and local governments. Leading up to its passage were decades of violent denial of the vote to African Americans in the South and to Latinos in the southwest United States. The Voting Rights Act is often considered by historians as the most successful civil rights legislation ever enacted.

These acts prohibit discrimination based on race, color, religion, or national origin. Of course, the passing of these acts didn't end discrimination overnight, but they helped pave the way for minority groups to secure the rights and privileges awarded to all U.S. citizens.

You can be sure that the passing of these acts in the 1960s played an important part in Michelle's future husband, Barack Obama, becoming the first African American president of the United States!

two daughters, Malia and Natasha (Sasha). Family ties are important to Michelle, and she also still maintains a very close relationship with Craig and his family. Craig has said about Michelle,

*"My sister is a very warm and sympathetic person. When the chips are down, she and my wife are the people I talk to."*

Her family ties no doubt played an important role in her following Craig to Princeton University. Whatever the reason for getting her there, her next great educational adventure would be a life-changing one.

Michelle's mother Marian is a big part of Michelle's life, and lives in the White House with the Obamas.

# CHAPTER TWO

# New Experiences at Princeton

Michelle made honor roll during her four years at Whitney M. Young High School, yet her guidance counselor discouraged her from applying to Princeton University, claiming that her test scores weren't high enough. Luckily, Michelle didn't take this advice to heart. Her brother Craig was a sophomore at Princeton by then, and she had witnessed firsthand the process that he went through when applying to colleges. This would be one of the many times when Michelle's stubbornness and drive helped her overcome obstacles— no one was going to stop her from applying to Princeton.

She later said about Craig in regard to Princeton that, "I knew him. I knew his study habits, and I was like, 'I can do that, too!'" She knew that her scores weren't perfect, but she was very bright, a hard worker, and felt confident that she could impress in an interview.

Michelle was accepted to Princeton. In the fall of 1981, she began her first semester at one of the most prestigious Ivy League schools in the country.

## Coming Face to Face with Racism

When Michelle arrived at Princeton in 1981, only 16 percent of the student body were minorities. Michelle had grown up in a large black community, so she was, for the first time, different than most everyone else. Even though the administration at that time was trying to make up for discrimination in the past, racism was not rare at Princeton. The university had a long history of race problems, and entrenched racism is something that takes a long time to change.

Some professors and alumni of Princeton argued that African Americans weren't actually smart enough to be in Ivy League schools. Many believed that they had been allowed to attend only because of **Affirmative Action**. (In the 1960s, women were also the focus of this same debate. At the time, it was considered more difficult for women of any race to gain acceptance to Princeton.) After being immersed in the idealized world of Whitney M. Young High School, this came as a shock to Michelle.

Even though there were few outward signs of racism, there were many white students who resented the black students and avoided talking to them. These individuals

# Princeton University

Princeton University, located in Princeton, New Jersey, was founded in 1746 and is the fourth-oldest university in the nation. Nassau Hall, the single building where the college was contained for almost fifty years, was the site of Continental Congress meetings in 1783. Today, the university takes up nearly 500 acres (202 hectares).

Starting in the 1960s, Princeton made a concerted effort to attract the best and brightest students from underrepresented minority groups, including African Americans and women. Today, American minorities make up about 38 percent of the undergraduate student body. The founding of the Third World Center (now called the Carl A. Fields Center for Equality and Cultural Understanding), a place where minority groups could gather, socialize, and establish connections, was part of that effort.

As of 2013, Princeton had approximately 5,200 undergraduate students, and 2,600 graduate students. Noted graduates of Princeton include former president Woodrow Wilson, Nobel Prize-winning physicist Richard Feynman, former chairman of the Federal Reserve Paul Volcker, CEO of Hewlett-Packard Meg Whitman, and screenwriter and producer Ethan Coen.

felt that the African American students had been given special treatment, and were only accepted to Princeton because they were black.

This prejudice manifested in the social life at Princeton. One of the school's oldest traditions are its "eating clubs"—social clubs where students could socialize, dance, eat, of course, and make connections. These members-only clubs are similar to fraternities and sororities you find at many universities. A student could join the clubs only by invitation, and they have historically been whites-only. These clubs dominated Princeton's social life at the time. Michelle chose not to apply to any of these eating clubs, perhaps because she felt the "differentness" right away.

Ivy Club, Princeton University

The Ivy Club, established in 1879, is the oldest eating club at Princeton. Because these social clubs can be very exclusive, Michelle chose not to associate with them.

Later, in her senior thesis, Michelle would write, "My experiences at Princeton have made me far more aware of my 'blackness' than ever before. I have found that at Princeton, no matter how liberal and open-minded some of my white professors and classmates try to be toward me, I sometimes feel like a visitor on campus, as if I don't really belong." She continued, "It often seems as if, to them [her white classmates and professors], I will always be black first and a student second."

## New Friends and Social Clubs

True to her spirit, and following in her father Frasier's footsteps, Michelle didn't waste time dwelling on the negative aspects of Princeton. Michelle's social experiences at the university were based around the Third World Center, the purpose of which was "to provide, through intellectual and social activities, a setting and a program that will help minority students reinforce each other and also to create a forum for greater awareness and understanding among people of differing cultural backgrounds." (Some thought the original name was offensive to minority groups, and the center was renamed the Carl A. Fields Center for Equality and Cultural Understanding in 2002.)

The Third World Center essentially became an eating club for minority students. "The Third World Center was our life," said Angela Acree, Michelle's roommate during this time, "We hung out there; we partied there;

## What Is Affirmative Action?

Affirmative Action, which was introduced in the early 1960s in the United States, refers to the process of considering factors such as race, color, religion, sex, or national origin in order to help a previously underrepresented group in areas of employment, education, and business.

According to 2012 U.S. Bureau of Labor statistics, blacks are almost twice as likely as whites to be unemployed. The unemployment rate is also higher for Latinos than for whites. Blacks and Latinos also generally earn far less than whites. The latest U.S. Census Bureau Data shows that women earn 77 cents for every dollar that men earn, and Black and Latino women are the worst off of all.

According to the ACLU (American Civil Liberties Union), Affirmative Action is one of the most effective tools for fixing the injustices caused by the historic discrimination against women and people of color. Racism and sexism have existed in this country in one form or another for centuries, and it will take time and diligence to eradicate these wrongs.

Although most people these days feel that all people, regardless or color or gender, should have an equal chance to succeed, some feel that Affirmative Action isn't effective at achieving those goals. Some critics feel that it devalues the accomplishments of people who are chosen based on the social group to which they belong rather than their qualifications, thus making it counterproductive. Others argue that it replaces old wrongs with new wrongs, undermines the achievements of minorities, and encourages individuals to identify themselves as disadvantaged, even when they are not.

However, most people do agree that underrepresentation of minorities and women in positions of power and success is a long-standing and difficult problem that requires complex and multifaceted solutions.

we studied there." Michelle took a job at the Center, coordinating an after-school childcare program for the children of Princeton's lunchroom and maintenance staff. She made lifelong connections with some of the children and staff there.

Michelle enjoyed her experiences at the Third World Center, but realized that many of its members often ended up with a group of friends made up only of minority students. She and her friends sometimes wondered if such a center just served to drive a further wedge between the minority and white students. Is it better to assimilate or be separate? Is there some way to do both? Howard Taylor, one of Michelle's thesis advisors at the university, described Michelle's position on the question of isolation versus assimilation as moderate. "She was not an assimilationist, but she wasn't a wide-eyed militant either," he said. "She was able to straddle that issue with great insight." Thanks to her idyllic experience at Whitney Young High School in Chicago, Michelle knew there could be a better answer.

Perhaps in response to these concerns, Michelle also joined Stevenson Hall, which was an alternative student center opened in the 1960s in order to help open the university to new ideas. Stevenson Hall had a kosher kitchen and a large Jewish population, which exposed her to new friends and experiences she might not have otherwise had.

When friends and classmates discuss the Michelle they knew at that time, the person they describe is very similar to the person she is today: driven, academically ambitious, balanced, funny, and devoted to her family. On her yearbook page, Michelle included a personal message:

> *"There is nothing in the world more valuable than friendships. Without them, you have nothing."*

## Moving Beyond and Doing Her Best

Michelle knew she had been given an incredible opportunity, and she was determined to work hard and make the best of it. She finished her coursework early, and didn't allow herself to be intimidated by her professors. In fact, Craig called home at one point during Michelle's freshman year to complain about his sister. "Mom, Michelle's here telling people that they're not teaching French right."

Michelle's mom knew better than to get in the middle, and that this was Michelle's battle to wage. She told Craig, "Just pretend you don't know her."

Michelle majored in Sociology and minored in African American studies. She devoted herself to her studies and graduated *cum laude* (with distinction) in four years. Her thesis, entitled "Princeton-Educated Blacks and the Black Community," reveals some of the experiences she had while she was at Princeton. To research her thesis topic, she sent out 400 questionnaires to African American Princeton graduates about their feelings regarding race—and their interactions with black and white people—before and after attending Princeton. She wanted to know how these attitudes had changed during their college years. She asked about their Princeton experiences, and about their relationships with other African Americans.

The questions she posed included whether black graduates had become more or less interested in helping the black community after attending Princeton. What she found troubled her. The answers of the 100 or so alumni who responded indicated that as African Americans became more educated and achieved more success, they tended to move away from their identification with other African Americans.

In her thesis, Michelle wrote that she wanted to one day use her education and the opportunities she had been given to help the African American community. She would later spend a significant portion of her career doing just that.

## Looking to the Next Step

True to her ambitious nature and her high standards, Michelle decided to apply to law school as her next educational step. She didn't want to just be a lawyer, however. She wanted to attend one of the best and most prestigious schools in the country. So, after graduating from Princeton with honors in the spring of 1985,

Michelle
graduated
*cum laude*
from Princeton
in 1985.

Michelle set off to Cambridge, Massachusetts to begin
graduate studies at Harvard Law School. In addition to
a lucrative career and a passion for community work, this
road would eventually lead her back to Chicago, where
she would one day meet Barack Hussein Obama.

# CHAPTER THREE

# *Harvard Law School*

W hen Michelle arrived in the fall of 1985, Harvard was dealing with the same racial issues and tensions that she'd experienced during her years at Princeton. By this time, Michelle was twenty-one years old, more seasoned and experienced, and more comfortable in her own skin. This made the transition to Harvard not nearly as difficult as the one to Princeton had been. In fact, her law school adviser, Charles J. Ogletree, Jr., spoke in detail about where Michelle's mindset was at this point in her life.

"Princeton was a real crossroads of identity for Michelle," says Ogletree, "The question [for Michelle] was whether I retain my identity given by my African American parents, or whether the education from an elite university has transformed me into something different than what they made me. By the time she got to Harvard, she had answered the question." He went on to sum it up nicely:

> *"She [realized she] could be both brilliant and black."*

The question of how to define herself as a successful African American woman in a highly educated, mostly white world was one that was clearly important to Michelle. It was one that she asked herself and other blacks during her years at Princeton and Harvard. This was evidenced not only in her Princeton thesis, but also in the law she studied and the extracurricular activities she chose to participate in. Of course, Michelle wanted to be successful, and was enticed by the trappings of what an Ivy League education could bring. She said so herself.

"The thing about these wonderful schools," Michelle told reporter Rebecca Johnson, "is they can be surprisingly narrowing to your perspective. You can be a lawyer or you can work on Wall Street; those are the conventional options. They're socially acceptable and financially rewarding. Why wouldn't you do it?"

However, Michelle was called by her upbringing, and her own beliefs, to strive for something else. "She made a commitment to her father, who did not go to college, that she would pursue her talents to help her community," says Ogletree.

This very question—what should she do, what did she *want* to do, with her gifts, talents, and education—would gel and solidify during her time at Harvard.

## Studying the Law

Not long after starting at Harvard, Michelle called her former boss at the Third World Center at Princeton, Czerny Brasuell, and admitted, "If I could do this over, I'm not sure I would." It's not that she didn't like law school, she said, but perhaps she'd felt more comfortable doing meaningful work in the real world than she did having theoretical discussions in the classroom.

Despite her reservations, Michelle excelled in her studies and left an indelible impression on many of her professors, who remember her as a serious student who could form strong, convincing arguments to support her ideas. Although she was not as outspoken as others in her classes, she was not afraid to question authority. True to her personality and her track record, Michelle didn't always feel the need to speak up in class, but when she did it was usually to disagree with her professor.

One of Michelle's professors, David B. Wilkins, had this to say about his experiences with her: "Michelle was a student in my legal profession class, in which I ask students how they would react to difficult ethical and professional challenges... Many students shy away from putting themselves on the line this way, preferring to hedge their bets on deeply technical arguments that seem to absolve them from the responsibilities of decision making… Michelle had no time for such fig leaves. She always stated her position clearly and decisively."

Just as she had done at Princeton, Michelle quickly became involved in activities and causes that she believed in. Bringing to mind her Princeton thesis about Ivy League-educated blacks relating to and helping their communities, she recruited African American Harvard graduates to serve on the panel of the university's Black Law Students Association. The Harvard Black Law Students Association was a social club, but also served as an important support network, helping black students further their careers.

Michelle participated in demonstrations that called for Harvard to admit more minority students and hire more minority professors. She worked with the school's administration to recruit more African American students to attend Harvard. Michelle also joined the staff of Harvard's *BlackLetter Journal*, which focused mostly on how the law affected minorities. It was an alternative to the *Harvard Law Review* and other journals that were run mostly by white students.

Perhaps the most important part of her three years at Harvard Law School, though, was the time she spent working at the Harvard Legal Aid Bureau.

## Harvard University and Harvard Law School

Harvard University, located in Cambridge, Massachusetts, was founded in 1636 and is the oldest institution of higher learning in the United States. It was established by vote of the Great and General Court of the Massachusetts Bay Colony. Since its inception, it has grown from nine students with a single professor to an enrollment of more than 20,000 degree candidates, including undergraduate, graduate, and professional students.

The name Harvard comes from the college's first benefactor, the minister John Harvard of Charlestown. Upon his death in 1638, he left his library and half his estate to the institution. A statue of John Harvard stands today in front of University Hall in Harvard Yard, and is perhaps the University's best-known landmark.

Harvard Law School is considered one of the most prestigious law schools in the country. Many of its graduates have achieved important positions in the world, including the current Chief Justice of the Supreme Court, John J. Roberts, Jr. In fact, six of the nine current Supreme Court Justices are former Harvard Law School students.

Eight U.S. presidents have also attended Harvard University, including Theodore Roosevelt, Franklin Delano Roosevelt, John F. Kennedy, and Barack Obama—who, like his wife, attended Harvard Law School.

## The Harvard Black Law Students Association

The Harvard Black Law Students Association (HBLSA) was founded in 1967, and is now the largest chapter in the National Black Law Students Association. The purpose of the HBLSA is to provide support, guidance, and direction to black students in academic, professional, and social endeavors. Its main functions are to assist members in developing their legal careers and to provide opportunities for exposure to various aspects of the legal profession. It also provides a vehicle through which members' concerns are brought to bear on Harvard Law School policy and the community at large.

## Drawn Toward Community Service Work

Given her background, her interests, and her determination to help others, Michelle was a natural fit for the Harvard Legal Aid Bureau. The Bureau was made up of second- and third-year Harvard law students who provided free legal help to the disadvantaged citizens of Boston and the surrounding areas. Individuals who couldn't afford a lawyer could go to the Bureau, where the law students would help them file for divorce, handle conflicts with a landlord, get custody of their children, pursue their ex-spouses for back child support pay, and resolve Social Security disability benefit

disputes, among other issues. If the dispute ended up
in court, an experienced lawyer would likely help the
students, but otherwise the students ran their own cases.

Unlike the other organizations that Michelle joined
while at Harvard, the Bureau was multiracial. The students didn't come from the same backgrounds and races,
but they shared similar values and ideals. Their desire to
serve their community helped them form friendships.

Michelle spent a lot of time at the Bureau, and former
Bureau colleagues have described her as a compassionate,
dedicated lawyer. Ronald Torbert, president of the
Bureau at the time, said, "I remember being struck almost
immediately by—although she smiled a lot and we had a

Many students in law school participate in *pro bono* community work.

lot of fun—[how she had] a serious side to her, the things she thought about. She was very mature, very very bright; she handled some of the more complex landlord and tenant issues." He went on to say,

> *"I just remember her being very serious about the work she did, and she really cared a lot about the people she worked with."*

Michelle was a natural fit at the Harvard Legal Aid Bureau, where she spent lots of her time.

# The Harvard Legal Aid Bureau

The Harvard Legal Aid Bureau was founded in 1913 "for the purpose of rendering legal aid and assistance, gratuitously [free of charge], to all persons or associations who by reason of financial embarrassment or social position, or for any other reason, appear worthy thereof." As the nation's oldest student legal services organization, the Harvard Legal Aid Bureau aspires to be an engine for progressive change and social justice.

The Bureau is an entirely student-run, non-profit law firm currently composed of approximately forty second- and third-year Harvard Law School students. They specialize in four major areas of practice—housing, family, government benefits, and wage and hour law. (Family issues include divorce, child custody, visitation rights, paternity disputes, and support issues. Government benefits include such issues as appeals of the denial or termination of welfare, food stamps, unemployment, or Social Security disability benefits. Wage and hour law include nonpayment or underpayment of wages.)

The Bureau employs seven practicing attorneys who train students, accompany them to court, provide strategic advice, and assist in case management. Because the Bureau is student-run, students take the lead in exploring new potential practice areas.

## Choosing a Career Back in Chicago

As her time at Harvard drew to a close and Michelle was preparing to graduate, the question of what she wanted to do loomed large. Of course, she had been pondering this for a long time. In her Princeton thesis, she wrote, "… it is conceivable that my four years of exposure to a predominately white, Ivy League university has instilled within me certain conservative values," which might lead her to pursue "a high-paying position in a successful corporation." After all, she also had college loans to pay.

Harvard Law School allowed law firms and corporations to send representatives to campus for recruitment days, during which time these recruiters would lure students with promises of exciting, financially rewarding jobs. After speaking with representatives from one of these firms, Michelle's hard work and excellent grades paid off. She was offered a high-paying position with a private practice law firm called Sidley Austin LLP. Michelle had worked for this law firm the previous summer as a summer associate, which is similar to an internship, and had enjoyed it. When she was offered a position after graduation, she accepted. She knew what to expect at Sidley Austin.

Michelle began her career as part of the firm's marketing and intellectual property practice group in the summer of 1988. In addition to providing her a great salary, the job meant that Michelle would be returning to Chicago, and to her family and friends back home. It was also while at Sidley Austin that Michelle would meet another Harvard Law student by the name of Barack Obama.

For Michelle, her life choices often came back to family—family ties and family values. In the back of the Harvard Law School yearbook, parents could buy space to leave a message to their children who were graduating. In contrast to the sentimental and more formal messages left by other parents, Michelle's parents said to Michelle,

*"We knew you would do this fifteen years ago when we could never make you shut up."*

Michelle was on her way to becoming a high-paid, high-flying corporate lawyer. Thanks in large part to her family, she would always stay grounded.

# CHAPTER FOUR

# Life After Law School and Meeting Barack Obama

In 1988, Michelle returned to Chicago and began working at Sidley Austin LLP, a large corporate law firm. Her starting salary was $65,000—a relatively large amount of money at that time, especially for a first job. (In contrast, her father was making $40,000 after working for the city of Chicago for decades.) It meant that Michelle could begin paying off her student loans. She moved back into her childhood bedroom, and commuted to her office in the Chase Tower located in downtown Chicago. (At this time, her brother Craig was playing professional basketball in England for the Manchester Giants. He would return home later that summer and become a basketball coach.)

## Michelle as a Corporate Lawyer

Since Michelle had spent the previous summer as an associate at the firm, she was familiar with the kind of law they practiced. She was pleased when she was assigned to their marketing and intellectual property practice group. Many considered this department to be the least boring, most creative group in the company. Specializing in law that related to entertainment, their clients included advertising agencies, automobile companies, and celebrities.

According to Mary Carragher, Michelle's supervisor at the time, "It was the most fun area of practice in the firm, bar none. We were the coolest people, and we had the best work." She explained, "It was all popular culture stuff. You could do a lot of dull things in law, and this was—and still is, in my opinion—the best stuff."

Despite that reputation, Michelle found the work to be tedious sometimes. Sidley Austin didn't handle cases that were as soul satisfying as working for the legal aid clients at the Harvard Legal Aid Bureau had been. The head of her division, Quincy White, remembered this about Michelle:

*"She was extremely ambitious and wanted something that pushed her harder, something that was a more general challenge."*

Perhaps her boss was quick to pick up on Michelle's desire to do something that really mattered, because he also said that, "I couldn't give her something that would meet her sense of ambition to change the world." Despite this, her next case, which involved protecting the rights of Barney the purple dinosaur, did prove to be a good challenge for Michelle.

Michelle returned from law school to live in her childhood bedroom and commute to her office in downtown Chicago.

## Protecting the Purple Property

Sidley Austin represented the Corporation for Public Broadcasting, which had just purchased the **copyright** and merchandising rights to a purple dinosaur named Barney. *Barney & Friends* is a children's show featuring a purple dinosaur named Barney who walks upright and talks, conveying educational messages through song and dance. This show, aimed at preschool children, became an enormous hit.

## What Is Intellectual Property Law?

The American legal system provides rights and protections for owners of property. The kind of property resulting from mental labor is called *intellectual property*. These include books, articles, and other written works, as well as inventions, machines, and processes. The identifiable names and symbols of companies also fall into this category.

Rights and protections for owners of intellectual property, or IP, are based on federal **patents**, **trademarks**, and copyrights. Patents protect inventions of tangible things (such as a cell phone). Copyrights protect various forms of written and artistic expression (books, drawings, and paintings, for example). Trademarks protect a word, phrase, logo, or graphic symbol that identifies the source of goods or services (such as the Ronald McDonald clown).

The job of an IP lawyer is to help individuals or companies properly apply for legal protection of their intellectual property.

Michelle had frequently asked her division head, Quincy White, for more challenging projects. The managers at Sidley Austin knew that Michelle enjoyed working for good causes and they felt that assigning her this client would be a good fit. The firm was tasked with managing the trademark protection and distribution of *Barney* merchandise, as well as with negotiating with public television stations that wanted to broadcast the show. Michelle "had very little experience in that area," said one of her supervisors at the time, "but she latched onto it and did a very good job with it."

At the start of her second year at Sidley Austin, Michelle was given another seemingly routine task. She was assigned to mentor one of the new summer associates, a first-year Harvard law student with the unusual name of Barack Obama.

## Mentoring the New Summer Associate: What's All the Fuss About?

Although Michelle was committed to being a mentor to other law students, she was a bit wary about meeting Barack. There was a lot of buzz at the firm about him. Many of the lawyers said that he was a real standout at Harvard—intelligent, well spoken, thoughtful, and handsome. Some of Michelle's coworkers had already met Barack during the interview process and they thought there might be an attraction between the two of them. They egged her on, way before she even met him.

She later said this regarding the buzz she heard about Barack:

"He sounded too good to be true. I had dated a lot of brothers who had this kind of reputation coming in, so I figured he was one of those smooth brothers who could talk straight and impress people."

## Barack Hussein Obama

Barack Obama was born in Honolulu, Hawaii on August 4, 1961, to Stanley Ann Dunham and Barack Obama, Sr. A native of Kenya, Barack Sr. had been selected by the Kenyan government for a special program to attend college in the United States. He met Barack's mother Ann, who was raised in a small Kansas town, while they were both students at the University of Hawaii. They were married in 1961 and divorced when Barack was just two years old. Barack saw his father only once more after that. (His father died in a car crash in 1982 when Barack was twenty-one.)

His mother stayed and finished college after the divorce, and Barack was raised by his mother and maternal grandparents in Hawaii. He also spent four years of his life in Indonesia with his mother and his Indonesian stepfather. He graduated from Honolulu's well-respected Punahou School in 1979, and then attended Occidental College in Los Angeles for two years. He transferred to Columbia University in New York City in 1981, and graduated from there in 1983.

In 1985, he moved to Chicago to become a **community organizer**. He worked with people suffering job losses, helped to improve area schools, and sought out innovative ways to combat the high crime and unemployment rates in these neighborhoods. In 1988, he left Chicago to attend Harvard Law School, and graduated *magna cum laude* (with great honor) in 1991. He then returned to Chicago, where he would continue to pursue his work with community organizing and, eventually, enter politics.

Barack was older than the typical summer associate because he hadn't entered law school right after college. Sidley Austin had hired him as a summer associate after only his first year of law school, which was very unusual. Michelle just shook her head at all the talk, though. "I figured that they were just impressed with any black man with a suit and a job," she later said.

Despite her reservations, it was Michelle's job to make the new summer associate feel welcome, so she invited him to lunch on his first day. Right off the bat, she found he was easy to talk to and that he made her laugh. Michelle told journalist Katie Couric in a television interview years later,

*"Immediately I liked him because he was very bright, had a very interesting background—just a good guy to talk to."*

As she confided to Couric in the interview, she'd thought to herself, "This is a friend." They worked closely together that summer. Barack remembers that Michelle "even tried to set me up with a couple of her friends." Although he was immediately interested in Michelle, she kept the relationship on a professional level. She didn't think it was appropriate for her to date him, since she was his adviser. Nevertheless, Barack didn't give up.

Michelle resisted, but not because she wasn't interested. She had an unspoken policy at that time of not getting serious with any one man, or dating anyone for very long. "She fired them fast," her brother Craig said. "There would be no reason for me to dislike any of my sister's boyfriends... It was always more you felt sorry for them because you knew it was just a matter of time before they were getting fired."

Michelle was a driven woman, focused on her career. In fact, she told her mother during that time, "I'm not worrying about dating; I'm going to focus on me." Michelle also said that none of these men were ever as good as her father. She was waiting for someone who could meet the high standards he had set in her mind.

As she spent more time with Barack that summer, there were a few events that made her start to think perhaps there was more to him than she realized. Maybe, just maybe, he met that high standard.

## Wearing Her Down with His Charm

"Eventually, I wore her down," Barack wrote in his book *The Audacity of Hope*. After one of the company's employee picnics, Michelle drove Barack back to his apartment, and he offered to buy her an ice cream at Baskin-Robbins. They sat on the curb and talked about their childhoods. She found his childhood fascinating and exotic compared to hers, but Barack himself to be very down-to-earth. It was their first real, if impromptu, date. Barack says, "I asked if I could kiss her." After that, the two started dating in secret.

Although Michelle was cautious and acted aloof at first, it was clear to her close friends that she was falling fast. She called a friend from Harvard Law School, Verna Williams. "Guess what?" Michelle told her,

> *"I've got this great guy in my life. His name is Barack."*

As she told her friend how fascinating Barack was, Williams sensed that Michelle was crazy about this guy.

## Meeting the Family

Eventually during that summer, Michelle brought Barack over to meet her parents. Barack has written that he was immediately attracted to the warm, lively, close feeling in the Robinson household. In contrast to Barack's peripatetic, or nomadic, childhood, Michelle's was as traditional as it came. Barack has said that, "Visiting the Robinson household was like dropping in on the set of *Leave It to Beaver*," referring to a 1950s television show featuring an "ideal" nuclear family. In *Leave It to Beaver*, the father worked, the mother stayed home and cooked and cleaned, and the two boys never had any problems that their parents couldn't help them solve. Although he would sometimes tease Michelle about her near-perfect family, it was clear that he enjoyed their company. In fact, he immediately liked Michelle's parents.

Marian Robinson remembers Barack as being polite and low-key. But she doesn't remember too much about the first visit. Because of Michelle's track record of dumping previous boyfriends, they made an effort to not get too attached to him. Craig met Barack later that summer, after he was home from playing professional basketball in Europe. He got to know Barack, of all places, on the basketball court. Craig remembers being impressed with Barack's fortitude and confidence, both on the court and off.

As the family got to know Barack a little more that summer, they realized he was something special, just as Michelle had. He had a depth to him that wasn't apparent at first glance—perhaps he was a really good match for Michelle.

"My sister is one tough girl," Craig said. "I'm older and I'm still afraid of her. She's very accomplished, so she needs someone as accomplished as her. So, we in the family, we were just hoping that she could hang on to this guy, because it was readily apparent that he could stand up to her."

## Inspired to Make a Difference

Around the time that Michelle and Barack started dating, Barack took Michelle to a community meeting on the south side of Chicago, in the Altgeld Gardens neighborhood, where he had worked before law school as a community organizer. Barack spoke to the audience, mostly single African American mothers, in the basement of a church. As he spoke, Michelle watched as he transformed from a Harvard Law student in a stiff suit into a regular person, comfortable in his own skin, and able to relate to and inspire the people around him. She saw how the crowd connected with his passionate message. His message was moving, and it touched her.

Michelle has spoken emotionally about her feelings when she listened to Barack's speech that day. "People found something real and authentic in what he was saying, and it resonated with me." She continued,

> *"And I knew then and there that Barack Obama was the real deal."*

That day proved to be a turning point in their relationship. It would also serve as the spark that would reignite Michelle's own desire to make a difference in the world, and to give back to the community that helped raise her.

By the end of the summer of 1989, Michelle and Barack were a committed, romantic couple. As fate would have it, Barack was heading back to Cambridge to start his second year of law school, and Michelle was staying in Chicago. Neither knew how their relationship

Michelle and Barack became a committed couple during the summer
that he interned at Sidley Austin.

would endure the long-distance challenges they were
about to face.

Little did Michelle know, this would be the least
of the challenges facing her in the following months.
Several tragic, life-altering events were about to focus
Michelle's outlook and priorities as never before.

# CHAPTER FIVE

# *Careers and Passions*

By the end of the summer of 1989, even though Michelle and Barack were a committed couple, they had separate paths to take. Barack headed back to Cambridge to start his second year of law school at Harvard, while Michelle stayed in Chicago with her family and her job at Sidley Austin.

During his sophomore year, Barack continued to excel at Harvard, and was elected as the president of the *Harvard Law Review* (the first African American to receive this honor). Michelle, on the other hand, was finding work as a corporate lawyer less and less appealing. She was thinking more about following her passion and making a difference in her community.

Michelle and Barack fell into a comfortable long-distance relationship, exchanging letters and catching up through long-distance phone calls. During rare long weekends and holidays, they got together in Cambridge or Chicago. Life was moving along well for Michelle. That all changed in March 1990.

## Changing Perspectives

A terrible tragedy struck the Robinson family that March. Frasier, Michelle's father, died due to complications after a kidney operation. He was just fifty-four years old. Although he had been ill and had struggled with multiple sclerosis most of his adult life, his death came as a real shock to the family. Michelle was devastated.

At the point of Frasier's death, Michelle and Barack had been dating about six months. He flew back to Chicago to be with Michelle and her family at the funeral. In his book, *The Audacity of Hope*, he gave his perspective about this trying time in the Robinsons' lives:

*"As the casket was lowered, I promised Frasier Robinson that I would take care of his girl. I realized that in some unspoken, still tentative way, she and I were already becoming a family."*

Frasier's death also pushed Michelle to take stock and ask herself hard questions about what she was doing with her life. Was she giving back to her community? Was she using her career and education to benefit others like her? She later told *The New York Times* that when her father died,

> *"I looked out at my neighborhood and sort of had an epiphany that I had to bring my skills to bear in the place that made me. I wanted to have a career motivated by passion and not just money."*

Just a few months after her father's death, a dear friend of Michelle's died of cancer at the age of twenty-five. Michelle and Suzanne Alele were close friends from their Princeton days, and Michelle was at Suzanne's bedside when she passed away.

Driven by the reality of Suzanne's death, Michelle asked herself, "If I died in four months, is this how I would have wanted to spend this time?" At this point Michelle realized that she needed to give back, that she needed to do something she really loved and felt passionate about. She just had to figure out what that was.

## A Calling to Public Service

Michelle stayed at Sidley Austin until 1991, at which point Barack graduated from Harvard Law School and moved to Chicago. Barack was offered a full-time position at Sidley Austin, but he turned it down. Instead, he took a position with a small civil rights law firm. Shortly after Michelle began her search for a new job, she was offered a position on the staff of then-Chicago mayor Richard Daley.

Michelle accepted the job, which meant a considerable pay cut. However, this was her opportunity to work in the public service sector, something she hadn't done since her days at the Harvard Legal Aid Bureau. Her public service efforts would prove to be the driving force of her career.

Working for the mayor's office, Michelle became the economic development coordinator of the city's Department of Planning and Development. She helped solve problems that business owners were having with the local government. Michelle had little experience at the time. True to her nature, she jumped in with both feet and learned all she could—and, as before, she excelled. As a colleague of Michelle's in the mayor's office said about her,

*"She had this incredible ability to be a problem-solver. She was just totally unflappable."*

## The Ring Came with Dessert

As Michelle made the transition to a public service job, she and Barack enjoyed the fact that they were no longer a long-distance couple. They began to discuss marriage. However, there was a difference of opinion about whether marriage was important. Michelle, who had grown up with parents in a long-term, stable marriage, believed in it and wanted it for herself. Barack wasn't sold on the idea. He told Michelle that marriage didn't really mean anything; to him, the way you felt about someone was more important.

In an interview, she recalled telling him, "Look, buddy, I'm not one of those who'll just hang out forever. You know that's not who I am."

One night in 1991, Michelle and Barack went out for dinner at Gordon's, a fancy restaurant on Chicago's Clark Street, ostensibly to celebrate Barack's passing the Illinois bar exam (a law school graduate must pass this exam in the state where they want to practice law to prove their qualification). They were in the middle of yet another disagreement about marriage. When asked about this in an interview, Michelle remembered that she was feeling increasingly frustrated—but when the waitress brought out dessert, there was a box containing an engagement ring on her plate!

Michelle and Barack were married on October 3, 1992, at Chicago's Trinity United Church of Christ, where Michelle's brother Craig walked her down the aisle. The reception was held at the South Shore Cultural Center. After a honeymoon on the West Coast, they returned to Chicago, bought a condominium in Hyde Park, and settled into their marriage.

This family photograph of Michelle and Barack shows them on their wedding day in 1992 at Trinity United Church of Christ.

## New Jobs and Next Steps

Shortly after they were married, Michelle got a new job opportunity. In 1992, she took a job as the executive director of the Chicago chapter of a nonprofit called Public Allies. Public Allies prepares young people to take leadership positions in their communities, such as internships and jobs with nonprofits. One of their credos is that "anyone can lead." Michelle's new job involved getting the new chapter in Chicago up and running. She was tasked with recruiting college students and young people living in public housing projects to participate in the program.

## Chicago's Hyde Park Neighborhood

Hyde Park, located on the shore of Lake Michigan on the south side of Chicago, defies many stereotypes. Since its incorporation in the 1860s as a Chicago township, it has experienced a uniquely American metamorphosis and subsequent rebirth. During its first ninety years, Hyde Park was an exclusively white community. Racially restrictive covenants, which were formal rules and regulations prohibiting the sale of properties to minorities, kept African Americans from living there.

After the Supreme Court banned these covenants in 1948, Hyde Park was desegregated, and many black and Latino families moved there. As a consequence, many whites moved away (an unfortunate phenomenon called **white flight**). The neighborhood experienced economic decline. In the 1950s and 1960s, The University of Chicago, located in Hyde Park, spearheaded an urban renewal project. Old, dilapidated buildings were razed and new housing replaced them. The average income in Hyde Park soared during this time.

Today, Hyde Park is a prime example of a racially integrated middle-class neighborhood. The majority of its residents hold college degrees, and incomes are higher than in most other neighborhoods. Hyde Park is also home to several artistic and cultural centers, including many theaters and museums.

Through Michelle's leadership, the Chicago chapter of Public Allies was a success. It became a model for other chapters to emulate, a fact Michelle took as a personal accomplishment. During her four years there, she created a thriving and vibrant community of young leaders, and she helped the chapter raise funds to continue its mission. They even had a surplus when she left. As Public Allies' Paul Schmitz said, "She built it to last."

After her time at Public Allies, Michelle took the position of associate dean of student services at the University of Chicago in 1996. She created a community service program and organized student volunteers, similar to her work at Public Allies.

## Really? Politics?

As Michelle advanced her career and felt increasingly challenged and rewarded by it, Barack was experiencing some frustration with his own career. Increasingly, he came to the conclusion that to have a real impact, he would need to enter the world of politics. He told Michelle in 1995 that he wanted to run for an open seat in the Illinois state senate.

At first, Michelle was somewhat skeptical. Once she saw that this was something Barack really wanted to do, however, she supported his decision, helped him raise money, and attended campaign events. Thanks in part to Michelle's help, Barack won the election, and in January 1997, he was sworn in. Among other things, this meant he would be traveling to the Springfield capital three days a week, which was three hours from Chicago.

At that point, neither of them fully realized where this journey would lead. After an unsuccessful bid in 2000 for a U.S. House of Representatives seat, he became a U.S. Senator for Illinois in 2004. That same year, Barack would give the **keynote address** at the Democratic National Convention. This speech catapulted him into the national spotlight, and was a driving force that led to his White House bid in 2008.

It wasn't all smooth sailing right to the White House, though. With each campaign, Barack's choice to run for office was a difficult one for the couple to make, financially and otherwise. They both had student loan debt that they were still paying off, and running for office is an expensive endeavor. Furthermore, by this point they already had one child and wanted to have more. When Barack told Michelle that he wanted to run for the U.S. Senate in 2004, she was not on board.

Financially, she told him, "[Your career choice is] killing us... even if you do win, how are you going to afford this wonderful next step in your life?"

He replied, "Well, then... I'm going to write a book, a good book."

Being the practical person that she was, however, Michelle wasn't convinced.

They reached a low point in 2000. The couple had maxed out their credit cards to pay for Barack's unsuccessful congressional campaign. Barack purchased a cheap ticket to Los Angeles so he could attend the Democratic National Convention. When he arrived at the Los Angeles airport, his credit card was rejected by the car rental agency. Barack has spoken candidly about that time:

> *"I was broke. And not only that, but my wife was mad at me because we had this baby and I had made this run for Congress... It wasn't a high point in my life."*

In the end, it would be the royalties from Barack's two best-selling books, *Dreams from My Father* and

The Obamas bought this Georgian revival style, six-bedroom home in Hyde Park in 2005.

*The Audacity of Hope*, which would pull the Obamas out of their financial hole—and then some. He received a $2 million advance in December 2004 for signing the book deal. Proceeds from the books would eventually allow them both to pay off their student loans in full, as well as purchase a Georgian revival style, six-bedroom home in Hyde Park in 2005 for $1.65 million.

However, all that didn't start happening until 2004. Michelle and Barack still had a rough road to walk until then.

## Counting Her Blessings

Michelle's daughter Sasha was born just as Barack's political career was about to take off.

Six years into their marriage, the Obamas became parents. Anyone who knew Michelle knew that she had always dreamed of having her own family, but getting pregnant had proved difficult. Their first child, Malia Ann, was born on July 4, 1998. Their second daughter, Natasha, known as Sasha, was born three years later on June 7, 2001. Michelle slowly realized how these girls would change everything for her, in all the best ways. As she famously said many years later,

> "At the end of the day, my most important title is still mom-in-chief."

The parenting challenges that would lie ahead for Michelle weren't related to her commitment to her daughters—that was unwavering. For her, the biggest challenge would be letting go of the idea that there was only one way to be a happy family.

## Balancing Career, Family, and Politics

When Malia was born in July of 1998, the Illinois state senate was in recess, and Barack was on break from his teaching job at the University of Chicago. Michelle took three months' maternity leave. She got up with the baby in the mornings, and Barack took care of her at night. They shared the duties well, and enjoyed this special time.

Summer all too quickly turned into fall, however. Barack's recess in the legislature ended in September, and he was back to Springfield three days a week. When he was in Chicago, he spent a lot of his time focused on his teaching duties—attending meetings and grading papers.

The tension was already high between Barack and Michelle when Sasha was born in 2001, and things continued to slide even before Barack decided to try and run for the U.S. Senate seat. Michelle had pictured a life where her family sat down together for dinner every night. She felt cheated that her husband was gone all the time, leaving her to raise her two daughters alone. She was trying to balance her career and family, and she wanted a stable, two-parent home life for her daughters, like the one she herself had benefitted from. She told Barack that she had not married him in order to become a single parent.

Although he definitely wanted to do something to fix it, Barack couldn't understand why Michelle was so angry. It wasn't until years later that he had the hindsight to understand. "No matter how much I told myself that Michelle and I were equal partners," he said, "and that her dreams and ambitions were my own—the fact was that when children showed up, it was Michelle and not I who was expected to make the necessary adjustments."

## Choosing to Be Happy

Struggling to balance her career and caring for her daughters, and disappointed with Barack's absence, Michelle did consider becoming a stay-at-home mom. Her decision to continue working was a least partly a matter of finances. Before the book advance and royalties began easing the financial tension, her family needed the income. Michelle also enjoyed her career and knew that a part of her identity was wrapped up in it. However, something had to change.

After some soul-searching, Michelle realized that she could not change Barack. Instead, she needed to change her situation and accept Barack for who he was. "I spent a lot of time expecting my husband to fix things," she said. "But then I came to realize that he was there in the ways he could be. If he wasn't there, it didn't mean he wasn't a good father or didn't care." She went on,

> "I saw that it could be my mom or a great babysitter who helped. Once I was okay with that, my marriage got better."

Although the girls accompanied them on some campaign appearances, Michelle has been careful to protect their privacy.

Michelle made lots of small changes that helped her schedule and her attitude. She made time for herself by going to the gym at 4:30 a.m. Barack got up with the girls and fed them. She hired a housekeeper to help with laundry, cooking, and cleaning. She also enlisted her mother to help with childcare.

Just shortly after Sasha's birth, Michelle interviewed for a new job at the University of Chicago. Without another option, she was forced to take baby Sasha with her to the interview. However, despite this, she was offered the position and became the executive director for community affairs of the University of Chicago Hospitals. Her job was to help strengthen the relationship between the hospital and the south side community. It was a job she would love and excel at, and it came with a lucrative salary, which helped to ease their financial burdens. She finally felt she had balance in her life. She realized that she didn't want to be a crazy mother and an angry wife, and that meant putting herself first sometimes.

# CHAPTER SIX

# *Road to the White House and Her Legacy as First Lady*

Being a U.S. Senator meant that Barack spent his working days in Washington, D.C. He had wanted the entire family to move to Washington, but Michelle wanted to stay in Chicago, near her work, her mother, and the girls' school. So, instead of uprooting his family, Barack spent Tuesday through Thursday of each week in Washington and then flew home to Chicago on the weekends. This compromise on Barack's part allowed Michelle and the girls to remain in their new home in Hyde Park. Michelle was again shouldering the greater burden of the parenting duties, but she did not feel resentful anymore. She had figured out a way to make it work for her and her family.

In March 2005, Michelle was promoted to vice president for community and external affairs at the University of Chicago Hospitals. In addition to new responsibilities, the promotion came with a raise for Michelle. In her new capacity, she continued to help the hospital develop a relationship with the neighboring community. She increased volunteerism among staff and brought in community members to volunteer in the hospital. Ever pragmatic, she also developed a program that encouraged local residents to seek medical aid at the local clinic instead of waiting until the situation required emergency room care.

## Will He or Won't He?

After Barack gave the keynote address at the Democratic National Convention in Boston in July 2004, and then won the Illinois Senate seat a few months later, he and Michelle became celebrities. There was a lot of speculation in the media as to whether Barack would run for president in 2008.

Barack was coy, and evaded reporters' questions about a possible campaign. Behind closed doors, however, he clearly did want to run—but he needed to convince only one person: Michelle. She was understandably cautious. On several occasions, she met with the team who had helped Barack win the Senate race, and asked them many questions. How would they pay for the campaign? What would it mean for Malia and Sasha? How dirty could the campaign really get, and how would that affect their family life? Michelle was practical, and she was protective of her family. The team answered all her questions carefully and thoughtfully, and gradually she realized she needed to give Barack the go-ahead.

> *"Eventually I thought, This is a smart man with a good heart, and if the only reason I wouldn't want him to be president is that I'm married to him, no, I can't be that selfish."*

With Michelle officially on board, the hard work of running a presidential campaign began. When Barack formally announced his candidacy in February 2007, his campaign staff asked for Michelle's help. Michelle was articulate, smart, funny, and down to earth, and they wanted her out on the road helping Barack.

She agreed, but with many stipulations. She would never miss the girls' important events or games, and she would always be home by the time they went to bed. Some days she campaigned in New Hampshire in the afternoon, only to race home to Chicago by bedtime. Michelle also decided that she would need to step down from her position at the University of Chicago Hospitals. She would devote her time between the campaign and keeping things stable and consistent for her girls. It would be the first time she wouldn't be holding down her own job and making her own money. As the campaign went on, Michelle's mother Marian retired from her job to help Michelle care for her family full time.

Michelle took her job campaigning seriously. She was often called "the closer," thanks to her ability convince voters who were "on the fence" to vote for Barack. Her message was similar in content to Barack's, but she had her own, very honest way of speaking. Sometimes that got her in trouble, and she was even called unpatriotic once for speaking her mind. At other times, she would inspire everyone who was listening,

*"Barack and I... want our children—and all the children in this nation—to know that the only limit to the height of your achievements is the reach of your dreams and your willingness to work hard for them."*

## Yes They Can

In November 2008, the hard work of campaigning paid off. Barack Obama was elected the forty-fourth president of the United States—the first African American to hold the office. In January 2009, the Obamas moved to Washington, D.C. so that the girls could begin school at the start of the new semester. They lived in a hotel until the **inauguration** on

January 20, after which they moved into the White House. Grandmother Marian joined them to continue her support and help with the girls.

The Obamas celebrate Barack's election in Grant Park on November 4, 2008.

## First Priority: "Mom-in Chief"

As Michelle herself famously said, her most important role as First Lady is as "mom-in-chief." From the very beginning, she has made sure her daughters' lives are consistent and normal. For example, when the family first moved into the White House, Michelle told the White House staff that she wanted Malia and Sasha to do their own chores, such as cleaning their bedrooms and making their beds, just as they had always done. She and Barack also keep the girls out of the media spotlight as much as possible. Michelle and Barack sometimes refer to the girls when speaking publicly, and the Obamas are often officially photographed as a family, but Malia and Sasha themselves rarely give interviews. And, of course, Grandmother Marian resides in the White House to be there for the girls when Michelle cannot.

Malia and Sasha like to participate in White House lawn events held for local children.

Sasha and Malia have grown into teenagers during their years in the White House, and Michelle has worked tirelessly to keep them grounded and keep their priorities straight. Barack said it all during his 2012 acceptance speech:

*"Sasha and Malia, before our very eyes, you're growing up to become two strong, smart, beautiful young women, just like your mom."*

To Michelle Obama, her children are her greatest legacy. Motherhood is her first priority, and she has referred to the girls as "the heart of my heart and the center of my world." However, she also entered the White House as a First Lady—and planned to use the position to enact changes in the country that were near and dear to her heart, starting with childhood obesity.

## The White House Kitchen Garden

With the help of local elementary school students, Michelle planted her first kitchen garden on the White House's South Lawn in the spring of 2009. This was the first kitchen garden on White House grounds since First Lady Eleanor Roosevelt's victory garden during World War II.

Michelle had hardly any gardening experience, and wasn't sure about the soil and climate in D.C. Still, she wanted to plant the garden, she said, in order to "help bring a conversation about the food we eat, the lives we lead, and how all of that affects our children."

*"As both a mother and a first lady, I was alarmed by reports of skyrocketing childhood obesity rates and the dire consequences for our children's health."*

# *Victory Gardens*

Victory gardens were vegetable, herb, and fruit gardens planted in private residences and public parks in the United States during World War II (1941–1945) in an effort to reduce the demand on the public food supply, which was already under pressure due to the war effort. Citizens who planted victory gardens were seen to be aiding the war effort—doing so was a patriotic act and became part of daily life during the war.

According to Michelle's book, *American Grown, The Story of the White House Kitchen Garden and Gardens Across America*, Chicago led the nation in growing victory gardens. Her mother's family, in fact, had a plot in the local victory garden, which was on the corner of a vacant lot near their home. Her mother helped her grandmother tend to it, and they ate fresh fruits and vegetables from it. By the time Michelle and Craig came along, however, those gardens were gone.

Michelle and the White House garden staff used the victory garden model to demonstrate that this kind of local gardening could still be done, and had in fact been done successfully all over the country.

She knew from personal experience that it was difficult to be busy working parents and feed a family in a healthy way. Often families on a budget and with little time are forced to eat fast food or buy groceries that lack nutritional value. She wanted to set an example for other working families in the country. The garden signified her values and concerns and was her way to help bring about the change she wanted to see in the country.

The garden has been a great success, and White House chefs use produce from it for preparing meals for the First Family, as well as for official functions like state dinners. Some of the produce is donated to Miriam's Kitchen, a local homeless shelter that provides home-made meals and other services, as well as to soup kitchens near the White House. As of 2014, the garden was in its sixth successful year.

Michelle first planted the kitchen garden on the White House's South Lawn in 2009.

The success of the garden, and the outpouring of support from the nation regarding the issues of nutrition and obesity, inspired Michelle to start the *Let's Move!* campaign.

## Let's Move!

In February 2010, Michelle launched *Let's Move!*, a campaign to bring together community leaders, teachers, doctors, nurses, parents, and other family members in an effort to tackle the challenge of childhood obesity. On the same date, President Obama signed a presidential memorandum creating the Task Force on Childhood Obesity to review current programs and develop a national action plan.

The *Let's Move!* program's goal is to solve the problem of obesity in a generation, so that kids today grow up healthier than their parents and eventually raise their own children to be healthy. The program provides information to parents about healthy eating, helps to push schools to provide healthier choices in the cafeteria, encourages children to become more physically active, and strives to provide access to healthier foods for all families, regardless of socioeconomic status.

Michelle has been very involved with this initiative, and it's one she feels personally invested in.

*"In the end, as first lady, this isn't just a policy issue for me. This is a passion. This is my mission. I am determined to work with folks across this country to change the way a generation of kids thinks about food and nutrition."*

> ## Why Weight Matters: The Dangers of Childhood Obesity
>
> The U.S. government's Center for Disease Control and Prevention reports that childhood obesity has more than doubled in children and tripled in adolescents in the past thirty years. As of 2010 (the most recent published data), more than one third of American children and adolescents were overweight or obese. Why does this matter?
>
> Obese children have higher risk factors for cardiovascular disease, such as high cholesterol or high blood pressure, and are more likely to have prediabetes, a condition where high blood sugar levels indicate a high risk for developing diabetes.
>
> Children and adolescents who are obese are also more likely to be obese as adults, which puts them at risk for adult health problems such as heart disease, type 2 diabetes, stroke, osteoarthritis, and many types of cancer. In fact, obesity is on the verge of surpassing tobacco use as the leading cause of preventable death in America.

## *Joining Forces* in Support of the Military

In 2011, Michelle and Dr. Jill Biden (Vice President Joe Biden's wife) launched *Joining Forces*, an initiative to give military service members and their families opportunities and support, and to raise awareness of military families' unique needs regarding employment, education, and wellness.

Many veterans returning home from serving their country find it very difficult to return to civilian life, especially when it comes to finding a job. Culture gaps between civilian society and their military past often exist, and many employers don't see the relevance of military experience when hiring. Many servicemen and women also suffer from various degrees of Post Traumatic Stress Disorder (PTSD) and might seem like a risky investment to some employers. Still others lack the basic skills necessary to succeed in the job market; many veterans entered the armed forces directly after high school, and consequently don't have basic job-hunting skills. All of these factors and more contribute to an unemployment rate for veterans that is much higher than that of the general population.

*Joining Forces* works to combat these statistics by connecting servicemen and women, as well as veterans and military families, with the resources they need to find jobs at home.

Michelle and Jill Biden's goal was to raise awareness of this issue and recruit companies and organizations that would commit to hiring veterans. Michelle said in August 2012,

*"I want to send a very clear message to the men and women who are wearing—or who have worn—our country's uniform and to their spouses: when you have finished your service to our nation, you've got 2,000 great American companies ready and waiting to bring you on board."*

The program is still in its infancy, but it has already had a measure of success with increased hiring rates and the reduction of homeless veterans. For example, in December 2013, Phoenix, Arizona became the first city to reduce its chronically homeless number of veterans to zero.

*Joining Forces* is an active and ongoing project for Michelle.

## Her Legacy of Hard Work, Service, and Love

What can we learn from Michelle's legacy, her actions, and her attitude? It's important to work hard and reach your potential. The right attitude can make all the difference. You should always be yourself and stay true to your heart. It's important to give back to your community. The love of family can carry you through the rough times. The list is inexhaustible.

Any one of these wonderful lessons could stand as the legacy of an exemplary First Lady, but Michelle Robinson Obama has managed to embody them all with style and grace. What does the future hold for Michelle? What great acts of service and kindness are in her future? Perhaps her greatest legacy is that hard work and sacrifice can take you places—and one can only watch to see what Michelle tackles next.

# Timeline

**1985**

Graduates *cum laude* from Princeton University

**1989**

Mentors intern named Barack Obama at Sidley Austin

**1996**

Works as associate dean of student services for the University of Chicago

**1964**

Born January 17 in Chicago, Illinois

**1986**

Works for Harvard Legal Aid Bureau

**1992**

Marries Barack Hussein Obama on October 3 at Chicago's Trinity United Church of Christ

Accepted to gifted student program at Bryn Mawr Elementary School in Chicago

**1975**

Graduates from Harvard Law School and starts job at Sidley Austin LLP in Chicago in the law firm's marketing and intellectual property practice group

**1988**

Founds the Chicago branch of Public Allies, which encourages young people to serve in their communities (this branch becomes a model for others around the country)

**1992**

Accepted to Harvard Law School

**1985**

Michelle's father, Frasier Robinson, dies at age fifty-four of complications from kidney surgery

**1990**

**2001**

Becomes executive director for community affairs of the University of Chicago Hospitals

**2009**

On January 20, Michelle and family move into White House

**2000**

Barack runs unsuccessfully for U.S. House of Representatives seat; campaign drains the family's finances

**2007**

Barack announces his presidential candidacy in Springfield, Illinois

**2011**

Michelle and Dr. Jill Biden launch *Joining Forces.*

Daughter Natasha (Sasha) Obama born on June 10

**2001**

Barack elected 44th president of the United States, and becomes first African American president

**2008**

Barack wins reelection for second term as president

**2012**

Daughter Malia Ann Obama born on July 4

**1998**

Promoted to vice president for community and external affairs at the University of Chicago Hospitals

**2005**

Launches *Let's Move!*

**2010**

# SOURCE NOTES

## CHAPTER 1

P. 6, Obama, Michelle, Democratic National Convention Address, October 25, 2008. Transcript from www.nytimes.com, August 26, 2008. Retrieved February 3, 2014 from http://elections.nytimes.com/2008/president/conventions/videos/20080825_OBAMA_SPEECH.html

P. 6, Obama, Democratic National Convention Address, October 25, 2008.

P. 6, Obama, Democratic National Convention Address, October 25, 2008.

P. 6, Obama, Democratic National Convention Address, October 25, 2008.

P. 9, Obama, Democratic National Convention Address, October 25, 2008.

P. 10, Obama, Democratic National Convention Address, October 25, 2008.

P. 12, Obama, Democratic National Convention Address, October 25, 2008.

Pp. 12–13, Jay Newton-Small, "Michelle Obama Finds Her Voice Too," *Time*, January 24, 2008.

P. 13, Slevin, Peter, "Her Heart's in the Race," *Washington Post*, November 28, 2007.

P. 13, Obama, Democratic National Convention Address, October 25, 2008.

P. 15, Collins, Lauren, "The Other Obama: Michelle Obama and the Politics of Candor," *The New Yorker*, March 10, 2008.

P. 15, Collins, "The Other Obama: Michelle Obama and the Politics of Candor."

P. 17, Robinson, Craig, Democratic National Convention Address, August 25, 2008. Transcript from chicago.about. com.

P. 18, Obama, Michelle, Primary Campaign Stump Speech, Durham, North Carolina, May 2, 2008. www.c-span. org, May 2, 2008. Video retrieved February 3, 2014 from http://www.c-span.org/video/?205147-1/Durh

P. 20, Johnson, Rebecca, "Michelle Obama's the Natural," *Vogue*, September, 2007.

# CHAPTER 2

Pp. 23–24, Wolffe, Richard, "Barack's Rock," Newsweek, February 25, 2008.

P. 27, Obama, Michelle, "Princeton-Educated Blacks and the Black Community," 1985. Retrieved February 3, 2014 from http://www.politico.com/pdf/080222_MOPrincetonThesis_1-251.pdf

P. 27, Snowden, Conrad D., "The Third World Center," from Alexander Leitch, *A Princeton Companion*, Princeton University Press (1978). Retrieved February 3, 2014 from http://etcweb.princeton.edu/CampusWWW/Companion/third_world_center.html

P. 30, Jacobs, Sally, "Learning to Be Michelle Obama," *Boston Globe*, June 15, 2008.

P. 30, Breger, Esther, "All Eyes Turn Toward Michelle Obama '85," *Daily Princetonian*, November 5, 2008.

P. 31, Lightfoot, Elizabeth, *Michelle Obama, First Lady of Hope* (Guilford, CT: The Lyons Press, 2009), p. 170.

P. 31, Collins, "The Other Obama: Michelle Obama and the Politics of Candor."

P. 31, Collins, "The Other Obama: Michelle Obama and the Politics of Candor."

# CHAPTER 3

Pp. 35–36, Jacobs, "Learning to Be Michelle Obama."

P. 36, Jacobs, "Learning to Be Michelle Obama."

P. 36, Johnson, Rebecca, "Michelle Obama's the Natural," *Vogue*, September, 2007.

P. 36–37, "Michelle Obama's Commitment to Public Service Began at HLS," *Harvard Law School Spotlight*, December, 2013. Retrieved February 3, 2014 from http://www.law.harvard.edu/news/michelle-obama-at-hls.html

P. 37, Mundy, Liza, *Michelle: A Biography* (New York, NY: Simon & Schuster, 2008), p. 78.

Pp. 37–38, Saulny, Susan, "Michelle Obama Thrives in Campaign Trenches," *The New York Times*, February 14, 2008.

P. 40, Harvard Black Law Students Association (HBLSA) website, "About Us." Retrieved February 3, 2014 from http://www3.law.harvard.edu/orgs/blsa/about/

Pp. 41–42, Mundy, *Michelle: A Biography*, p. 84.

P. 42, Mundy, *Michelle: A Biography*, p. 84.

P. 43, Harvard Legal Aid Bureau website, "About Us." Retrieved February 3, 2014 from http://www.harvardlegalaid.org/about-us

P. 44, Robinson, Michelle LaVaughn, "Princeton-Educated Blacks and the Black Community," 1985. Retrieved February 3, 2014 from http://www.politico.com/pdf/080222_MOPrincetonThesis_1-251.pdf

P. 45, Mundy, *Michelle: A Biography*, p. 85.

## CHAPTER 4

P. 48, Mundy, *Michelle: A Biography*, p. 90.

P. 48, Mundy, *Michelle: A Biography*, p. 92.

P. 49, Mundy, *Michelle: A Biography*, p. 92.

Pp. 50–51, Quoted in Mundy, *Michelle: A Biography*, p. 92.

P. 51, David, Mendell, *Obama: From Promise to Power*. (New York, NY: Amistad, 2007) pp. 93-94.

P. 54, Mendell, *Obama: From Promise to Power*, pp. 93-94.

P. 54, *CBS Evening News with Katie Couric*. Broadcast February 15, 2008. Retrieved February 3, 2014 from http://www.cbsnews.com/videos/michelle-obama-speaks/

P. 54, *CBS Evening News with Katie Couric.*

P. 54, Obama, Barack, *The Audacity of Hope*, (New York, NY: Crown, 2006) p. 329.

P. 55, Bakst, Charles M., "Brown Coach Robinson a Strong Voice for His Brother-in-Law Obama," *Providence Journal*, May 20, 2007.

P. 55, Quoted in Cassandra West, "Her Plan Went Awry, But Michelle Obama Doesn't Mind," *Chicago Tribune*, September 1, 2004.

P. 55, Obama, *The Audacity of Hope*, p. 330.

P. 55, Obama, *The Audacity of Hope*, p. 330.

P. 56, Parsons, Christi, Bruce Japsen, and Bob Secter. "Barack's Rock," *The Chicago Tribune*, April 22, 2007.

P. 56, Obama, *The Audacity of Hope* (Kindle edition).

P. 57, Reynolds, Bill, "Welcome to Obama's Family," *Providence Journal*, February 15, 2007.

P. 58, Kornblut, Anne E., "Michelle Obama's Career Timeout," *Washington Post*, May 11, 2007.

P. 58, Kornblut, "Michelle Obama's Career Timeout."

# CHAPTER 5

P. 62, Obama, *The Audacity of Hope*, p. 332.

P. 63, Powell, Michael, and Jodi Kantor, "After Attacks, Michelle Obama Looks for a New Introduction," *The New York Times*, June 18, 2008.

P. 63, Wolffe, "Barack's Rock."

P. 64, Parsons, Japsen, and Secter. "Barack's Rock."

P. 65, Collins, "The Other Obama: Michelle Obama and the Politics of Candor."

P. 68, Parsons, Japsen, and Secter, "Barack's Rock."

P. 69, Mendell, *Obama: From Promise to Power*, p. 99.

P. 69, Mendell, *Obama: From Promise to Power*, p. 99.

P. 70, Mendell, *Obama: From Promise to Power*, p. 144.

P. 72, Obama, Democratic National Convention Address, October 25, 2008.

P. 73, Obama, *The Audacity of Hope*, p. 341.

P. 74, Johnson, "Michelle Obama's the Natural."

P. 74, Johnson, "Michelle Obama's the Natural."

# CHAPTER 6

P. 79, Melinda, Henneberger, "Michelle Obama Interview: Her Father's Daughter," *Reader's Digest*, October, 2008.

P. 80, Obama, Democratic National Convention Address, October 25, 2008.

P. 81, Obama, Democratic National Convention Address, October 25, 2008.

P. 82, Obama, Barack, 2012 Presidential Acceptance Speech, November 7, 2012. Transcript retrieved February 3, 2014 from http://www.whitehouse.gov/the-press-office/2012/11/07/remarks-president-election-night

P. 83, Obama, Democratic National Convention Address, October 25, 2008.

P. 83, Obama, Michelle, *American Grown: The Story of the White House Kitchen Garden and Gardens Across America*, (New York, NY: Crown, 2012) pp. 9–10.

P. 83, Obama, *American Grown: The Story of the White House Kitchen Garden and Gardens Across America*, pp. 9–10.

P. 86, *Let's Move* website. Retrieved February 3, 2014 from http://www.letsmove.gov/about

P. 87, Centers for Disease Control and Prevention, "Childhood Obesity Facts." Retrieved January 31, 2014 from http://www.cdc.gov/healthyyouth/obesity/facts.htm

P. 88, *Joining Forces* website. Retrieved December 20, 2013 from http://www.whitehouse.gov/joiningforces

# GLOSSARY

**Affirmative Action** The process of considering factors such as race, color, religion, sex, or national origin in order to help a previously underrepresented group in areas of employment, education, and business.

**civil rights** The rights of personal liberty given to U.S. citizens by the thirteenth and fourteenth amendments to the U.S. Constitution and by acts of Congress.

**community organizer** A person who works with neighbors, local community leaders, and others with self-interest to address issues plaguing their community or neighborhood.

**convention** A meeting of the delegates of a political party in order to create a platform and select candidates for office.

**copyright** Intellectual property law protecting various forms of written and artistic expression (books, drawings, and paintings, for example).

**Democratic Party**  One of the two major contemporary political parties in the United States, along with the Republican party. The modern Democratic Party was founded around 1828 and is the oldest political party in the world. Since the 1930s, the party has promoted a socially liberal and progressive platform.

**Great Migration**  The movement of approximately six million African Americans from the rural South to large northern cities in search of better jobs and fairer treatment. It spanned from 1910 to 1970, and changed the landscape of many of America's large northern cities, including Detroit, Philadelphia, New York, and Chicago.

**inauguration**  The ceremony to officially induct someone into office. In the United States, the presidential inauguration day is January 20th.

**Jim Crow Laws**  Rules in the American South between 1876 and 1965 that mandated the legal separation of blacks and whites. This included separation in schools, public restrooms and parks, restaurants, drinking fountains, and in public transportation.

**keynote address**  A speech given to present the primary issues to the listening crowd, as well as to induce unity and enthusiasm.

**multiple sclerosis (MS)**  A degenerative, autoimmune disease that attacks the central nervous system (the brain and spinal cord). People with MS suffer from muscle tremors and general muscle weakness and numbness, sometimes leading to paralysis. It generally gets worse over time and there is no known cure.

**patent**  Intellectual property law protecting inventions of tangible items, such as a light bulb.

**precinct captain**  An elected officer in a political party who serves as a direct link between the party and the voters in his local district. The job involves facilitating voter registration, leading voter-outreach projects, handing out campaign and party information, and addressing general voter concerns.

**segregation**  The separation or isolation of a race, class, or ethnic group by barriers to social interaction, separate educational facilities, or other discriminatory means.

**trademark**  Intellectual property law protecting a word, phrase, logo, or graphic symbol that identifies the source of goods or services, such as the Apple Inc. logo.

**white flight**  The departure of white families, usually from urban neighborhoods undergoing racial integration or from cities implementing school desegregation.

# FURTHER INFORMATION

## Books

Branch, Taylor. *The King Years: Historic Moments in the Civil Rights Movement.* New York, NY: Simon & Schuster, 1998.

Jones, LeAlan, Lloyd Newman, and David Isay. *Our America: Life and Death on the South Side of Chicago.* New York, NY: Simon & Schuster, 1997.

Obama, Barack. *The Audacity of Hope.* New York, NY: Crown, 2006.

Obama, Barack. *Dreams from My Father.* New York, NY: Crown, 2004.

Obama, Michelle. *American Grown: The Story of the White House Kitchen Garden and Gardens Across America.* New York, NY: Crown, 2012.

Wilkerson, Isabel. *The Warmth of Other Suns: The Epic Story of America's Great Migration.* New York, NY: Vintage Books, 2010.

## Websites

### Civil Rights Act of 1964

www.judiciary.senate.gov/about/history/CivilRightsAct.cfm

A summary of the passing of the Civil Rights Act, what it includes, how it came about, timelines, and more.

### Joining Forces

http://www.whitehouse.gov/joiningforces

Website for Michelle Obama and Dr. Jill Biden's *Joining Forces*, an initiative to give military service members and their families opportunities and support, and to raise awareness of military families' unique needs regarding employment, education, and wellness.

### United States White House

www.whitehouse.gov

The United States White House official website. Visit for current videos and articles about all things presidential. Includes an Issues page, information about the administration, and historical information. First Lady Michelle Obama has her own link on the page.

## DVDs

*Biography: Barack Obama*
A&E Home Video. Distributed by New Video, © 2007.

Cable-television biography about the life of Illinois senator Barack Obama, made before he began campaigning to be the Democratic party's candidate for the 2008 presidential race.

*By the People: The Election of Barack Obama*
HBO Documentary Films. Distributed by Sony Pictures Home Entertainment, © 2010.

This 2009 documentary film follows Barack Obama and various members of his campaign team, including David Axelrod, through the two years leading up to the United States presidential election on November 4, 2008.

# BIBLIOGRAPHY

"About Harvard Law School." www.law.harvard.edu. Retrieved December 2, 2013 from www.law.harvard. edu/about/index.html

"About the ACLU." www.aclu.org Retrieved December 20, 2013 from www.aclu.org/about-aclu-0

"American Intellectual Property Law Association." www. aipla.org. Retrieved December 17, 2013 from www. aipla.org/about/who/Pages/default.aspx

Bodden, Valerie. *Michelle Obama, First Lady & Role Model*. Edina, MN: ABDO, 2010.

Brophy, David Bergen. *Michelle Obama: Meet the First Lady*. New York, NY: HarperCollins, 2009.

"Chicago's Hyde Park Historical Society." www. hydeparkhistory.org. Retrieved December 15, 2013 from www.hydeparkhistory.org/

Colbert, David. *Michelle Obama: An American Story*. Boston, MA: Houghton Mifflin Harcourt, 2009.

Collins, Lauren. "The Other Obama: Michelle Obama and the Politics of Candor," *The New Yorker*, March 10, 2008. www.newyorker.com/ reporting/2008/03/10/080310fa_fact_ collins?currentPage=all

"First Lady Michelle Obama: The White House." www.whitehouse.gov. Retrieved December 21, 2013 from www.whitehouse.gov/administration/first-lady-michelle-obama

"Harvard Black Law Students Association." www3.law.harvard.edu/orgs/blsa/. Retrieved December 3, 2013 from www3.law.harvard.edu/orgs/blsa/

"Harvard Law Review." www.harvardlawreview.org. Retrieved December 4, 2013 from www.harvardlawreview.org/index.php

Harvard Legal Aid Bureau. "About Us." www.harvardlegalaid.org. Retrieved December 3, 2013 from www.harvardlegalaid.org/about-us

Johnson, Rebecca. "Michelle Obama's the Natural," *Vogue*, September, 2007. www.vogue.com/magazine/article/michelle-obama-the-natural/#1

Kornblut, Anne E. "Michelle Obama's Career Timeout," *Washington Post*, May 11, 2007. www.washingtonpost.com/wp-dyn/content/article/2007/05/10/AR2007051002573.html

Lightfoot, Elizabeth. *Michelle Obama, First Lady of Hope.* Guilford, CT: The Lyons Press, 2009.

Mendell, David. *Obama: From Promise to Power.* New York, NY, Amistad, 2007.

Mundy, Liza. *Michelle: A Biography.* New York, NY, Simon & Schuster, 2008.

Obama, Barack. *The Audacity of Hope.* New York, NY: Crown, 2006.

Obama, Barack. *Dreams from My Father*. New York, NY: Crown, 2004.

Obama, Michelle. *American Grown: The Story of the White House Kitchen Garden and Gardens Across America.* New York, NY: Crown, 2012.

"Recess Reading: An Occasional Feature From The Judiciary Committee: The Civil Rights Act of 1964." www.judiciary.senate.gov. Retrieved November 19, 2013 from www.judiciary.senate.gov/about/history/ CivilRightsAct.cfm

Swarns, Rachel L. *American Tapestry: The Story of the Black, White, and Multiracial Ancestors of Michelle Obama*. New York, NY: HarperCollins, 2012.

"U.S. Bureau of Labor Statistics: Race and Unemployment." www.bls.gov Retrieved December 10th, 2013 from www.bls.gov/cps/cpsaat05.htm

"The US Department of Justice: Voting Rights Act of 1965." Retrieved November 19, 2013 from www. justice.gov/crt/about/vot/intro/intro_b.php

Wheeler, Jill C. *Michelle Obama, First Ladies*. Edina, MN: ABDO, 2010.

Wilkerson, Isabel. *The Warmth of Other Suns: The Epic Story of America's Great Migration*. New York, NY: Vintage Books, 2010.

Wolffe, Richard. "Barack's Rock," *Newsweek*, February 25, 2008.

# INDEX

# ABOUT THE AUTHOR

**Kezia Endsley** has edited hundreds of books over the years, and written a few articles and papers as well. This is the first book she has written. It makes sense that her inaugural book would be about Michelle Obama, since she became an ardent supporter of Barack Obama and his wife after hearing him speak in 2007. She campaigned and canvassed for his run for the White House in her hometown of Indianapolis, Indiana. Kezia, like Michelle, learned early on that being active in politics was important from her parents' involvement in their local Democratic party. She hopes her daughter and two sons will develop a passion for politics as well someday.